Praise for
Echoes from the Stars

"*Echoes from the Stars* is a brilliant rendition of an ancient tale about creation told throughout the world. A well-crafted blend of journeys that take you deeply into process and discovery and imaginative poetry, Beth offers us a moving narrative about one-ness with all life. Read, discover, journey and enjoy!"

— Alberto Villoldo, Ph.D., Bestselling Author of *Shaman, Healer, Sage* and *One Spirit Medicine*

"This illuminating book led me into realms I had not explored."
— J. Don Vann, Ph.D., University of North Texas Regents' Professor, Professor Emeritus in English

"A delightful read filled with impassioned landscapes of love and spirit. Beth's magical word crafting is uplifting, generous, and compassionate."
— Jose Luis Herrera, Founder, Rainbow Jaguar Institute and Chairperson, Andean Research Institute

"These stories are eminently valuable and all the richer for being wrapped in fable."
— Christine Irving, Poet and Author of *Magdalene, A.D.*

Also by Beth Honeycutt

Finding Direction

Echoes from the Stars

by BETH HONEYCUTT

Copyright @2017 Beth Honeycutt.

All rights reserved. No part of this book may be reproduced or transmitted in any form or by any means, electronic, mechanical, photocopying, recording, or otherwise, without the express written permission of the publisher except for the use of brief quotations in a book review. Send any inquiries to

Beth Honeycutt
The Calming Center, Publisher
1811 Greenwood Drive
Denton, TX 76209
www.TheCalmingCenter.com

Library of Congress Control Number: 2017904728
Beth Honeycutt, Denton, TX

ISBN-13: 978-0692857748
ISBN-10: 0692857745

Honeycutt, Beth.

Echoes from the Stars / Beth Honeycutt

Book Layout and Design @2017 by Tonya Littmann
Cover art @2017 by Zarina Karapetyan
Photography @2017 by Stephanie Honeycutt, Denton, Texas

Printed in the United States of America.

Dedicated

To adventurers of place, space, and time
who stand at the precipice of new ways to understand
this wondrous expression called life –
and who, when the wind blows, spread their wings and fly.

Contents

Preface		1
1	Invitation	3
2	The People of the Stars	6
3	The Mountains	8
4	Connection	14
5	The Waters	17
6	Dreaming Beside You	22
7	Another Beginning	28
8	Inner Lights	33
9	Wandering	39
10	Breathing	43
11	Grounding	49
12	Climbing at the Center	55
13	A Collective	62
14	Skins for Ceremonies	67
15	First Tree	73
16	Standing	80
17	Inside the Moon	85
18	Leaning	92
Epilogue		94
Chapter Notes		96
Acknowledgments		97
Glossary		99
Reflections and Insights		101
Note From the Author		103

Echoes from the Stars

Preface

I grew up in a family of storytellers. I was an adult, however, when I became aware of depth gained from the conscious use of my breath when speaking, whether telling stories, giving presentations, or raising two children. While that first inhale is what brings us life as infants, every subsequent breath is an opportunity to return to an alertness in which we fully express being present. Exercising my voice as speaker, parent and poet, I found myself listening to the magic between the movements of the breath.

In these moments between breaths, my awareness of a fresh perspective of our historical birthing first came to light.

Echoes from the Stars, a retelling of the creation story, draws on elements of Andean cosmology interwoven with the physical evolution of the Earth from barren rock to Eden. A female interpreter speaks before a council of supernatural beings to save the Earth. Her voice tells a spiritual story, even as her poems speak of humanity.

As you move into these pages, I invite you to be involved in the poems, stories, and meditations. Experience the short pieces as the greater story unfolds and be part of the processes, for they are cloaks in which to be wrapped on journeys inward. Participate with your inner vision and ability to dream as well as with your physical body, affirming the path is yours to imagine and populate. Trust your inner knowing and give yourself permission to take what you need from the writings, setting your own pace for the reading and reflection.

Having traveled the sacred mountains in Peru with some of the indigenous Q'ero shamans, I borrow a few words from these Earthkeepers. In the Quechua language for instance, the word *chaska* means star, and the suffix *-kuna* makes a singular word plural, so the word *chaskakuna* refers to the collective spirit of the star people. When you read of the Chaskakuna, know the reference is to those early Beings who arrived from the center of Creation, the People of the Stars.

Taste pictures in the poetry on the tongue of your imagination. Allow feelings to resonate in your bones. Flow with the unfolding of a new landscape, and if your belief system is without an experience of the realm of the spirit, lend this book an openness that allows your heart to understand before your head.

Choosing to live with differing perspectives encourages growth and an experience of life's fullness. Be present to insights that are physical, emotional, mental, and spiritual. May you find within moments of unexpected joy.

1 Invitation

Come, sit in a circle while I remember this story with you.
The story begins with breath.
That's right. Inhale. Exhale.
Breathe.
The breath carries with it the completeness of the story, so make sure you breathe from your belly and not your chest. Access all of the color, the heart, of what I tell you.
Listen to the rhythm of the wind of the telling.
Open yourself to the first times, the newest of places, where a sense of freshness unfolds just for you...and you...and you. Hold no expectations; carry no external thoughts.
Feel the words take you back now to the earliest of places upon this young planet before there was time.

Called to Accountability

One Who Breathes the Wind guides me into a powerful energy vortex residing inside my *mestana*, the cloth holding my collection of healing stones. From there, I lift upward as if transported into the air before being thrust downward into curving tunnels which head out into the galaxies, the stars, the multiverse, to the very Place of Beginnings.

I feel set down with great precision.

I wait beside the platform where individuals stand to be heard before a council of Gods, many dimensions of the One Source. There are innumerable Beings gathered in front of me and circled around the platform. Called to speak, I shake the nervousness out of my clammy hands. I walk up six steps to the podium to address these Luminaries about Earth, about Gaia.

At first, I do not know what to say. Talking in general terms about humankind, how though we might be industrious, we could use more hope and peace, sounds contrived and trivial. I wonder how to convey anything new to these gods and feel a wave of inadequacy.

Then I recall the unusual direction of a recent conversation. The spirits of the Ancient Grandmothers told me that while spiritual beings have no body sensations like touch or taste or smell, they do still remember.

That is the key: I realize my words mean nothing to these disembodied spiritual energies unless they can remember the senses. With a calming and centering breath, I begin again in front of the Council.

I invite them to listen with me.

My words begin with a small, young stream as her water first springs down from a mountaintop, and we imagine these blue and white and clear cool waters moving with the land in gentling caresses upon the earth. The waters flow smoothly as they slide by rounded river stones or stop suddenly to hug large rocks before slipping around their choppy girth. Sometimes, the liquid strikes a boulder in rippling crashes causing the stream to splash on dragonflies and dampen translucent wings as these little ones continue their low-flying journeys above the waters.

Hummingbirds flit to the slower eddies beside the running liquid and hover in silence to drink their fill of the moving nourishment. Four-legged creatures bend to touch the life within the water, lips blowing prayers above the stream as tongues reach out to taste. The tiniest white, yellow, and fuchsia blossoms feed from the splattering runoff sprayed from the edges of this mountain stream, spreading in colorful clusters along the edges of the river widening and quickening its pace as it runs toward the ocean. The two-legged humans still learn of their dependence on this essence of water, but they honor its presence, its magnificent movement across the planet.

As I paint these word pictures, I plead for time for Earth, for hope, and for humanity. My words convey pictures of the planet these beings seek to know, for many of them remember her with great admiration.

My stories provide a shift in perceiving the changes experienced on the planet, and I sense a hunger for more.

These Star People want to know: Is Gaia still alive?

2 The People of the Stars

Envision with me an era before time when Earth was a barren landscape of plain shades of brown. What would the earth have heard before sounds were planted? There were only the stones to listen.

What would the rocks have felt in their inner darkness or under the floating diamonds of night? This was a period before the early greening cells of chlorophyll touched the earth with tints of organic life.

Although the land appeared to be still, the stones hummed deeply to themselves, sounds so long and slow and dark even the wind did not recognize them. Deep within the heart of each mountain that song continues to burn along deep burgundy paths to celebrate the beginning of each new day.

I bring you the stories I hear from the descendants of the Chaskakuna, those Beings of Light who arrived here after traveling the stars from the creative vortex which spiraled so far away and yet sent such imaginative pleasure to this barren world.

The Chaskakuna flew out from the central spinning where being began, bringing with them gifts for this new planet.

I catch their tales bringing joy and healing into the world.

Prepare to travel with me as we share the stories of the People of the Stars.

Sometimes the Mind Is a Deep Seasonal Storm*

Is cloud and lightning, thunder.
Is violent, as tornado winds are called,
howling in the folds of separation.

The rain's relentless pursuit of release
is a falling silver-flecked sphere
aimed toward rivers of connection.

And perception and story and belief?
As levees are, when breached by hurricanes or flooding waters.

3 The Mountains

Crunch.
Only sounds, and no one to hear.
Whooosh.
A wind, felt by the stones as a velvet pulsing. Pushing. Pulsing.
Mmmmmmmmmmm.

The stones are quiet across the flat plains of Earth. Boulders adjust themselves in their slow, heavy fashion upon the ground. Pebbles roll in slight "mmm's" before the graying wind, hot in the unencumbered light from the sun. The sand chips itself away from stone in order to catch more of the rays of brightness, loving how the glinting light on the crystalline flakes throws more shine to the spaces above.

Everything is still. Centered. The wisdom of the earth is deeply comfortable, nestled in the fallow in-between moments of creation.

When the first pair of far-flung lights arrive in the sky above this barren earth, they do not threaten. They hover as part of the Supreme Silence, shining brightly both by night and by day. These sky lights float in stillness, thoroughly acclimating and being accepted, radiating waves of energetic light that are met with similar light-waves from Earth. As the waves meet, the taller spires begin to envelop the planet in energetic sparks mapping out rivers of light that crisscross the silent globe.

While the lights in the sky dance upon the heavens, come together and slide apart, cavorting in luscious, breathless movements across the heavens, the stones pay attention. Resonating curiosity, stones the size of small hands exude a vibration as they begin exploring their environment with some of the smaller crystals leaning toward the moving lights, responding to an unseen magnetic pulse. Their rigorous movements alert some of the larger stones, and even the heavy boulders are not far behind, catching the feeling that something is changing. Something is preparing to shift.

The stones of the earth start rocking toward these sky lights, slowly, slowly, leaning into the pull of these moving balls of fire, yearning to be closer to the brighter beings in the heavens.

Along the flatness of the expanse of land across the globe, the rhythm of the rocks changes and builds in intensity. A deep-throated humming breaks through from below, at first a low vibration, before intensely reddened tones escape from cracking fissures in the ground as plates grapple and rise from their centers. Slipping above the land, mountains emerge after massive grinding and grating, pulling themselves upright in an excessive extension to reach the lights in the sky.

Following intervals of stretching and sliding amid intense negotiations, solid sheets of earth begin to tower over a flat horizon they once embodied. At the height of the scraping and groaning of the plates, some competing lighter stones agree to settle in the valleys and nestle in lower beds, while heavier boulders set themselves as pillars around the foothills of the newly-minted towering mountain ranges. A handful of peaks continue to rise skyward in a vain struggle to touch the lights in the highest of spaces, the land ever-striving to connect, to intimately know the lights, why they have come, what they are for, who they are, and the message they bring.

Lifting themselves toward the heavens atop the highest mountains on the planet, the last of the bare, dry stones rises. The plates stop shifting. A portal to one of the floating skylights in the heavens slips open.

The planet holds still.

No breath is drawn; no memory even of breathing yet is etched in the inner cells of the land.

Silence drapes softly over the non-expectant holding; no thoughts impact what happens.

The first of the Chaskakuna, those early Beings entrusted with creation, move out of that place above the land and descend to Earth in a liquid movement full of unspeakable joy. They spiral to the earth, unfold, and disappear under the fine silt of the newly-shifted land, opening the joining of the earth with the breath from this place beyond time where energy creates form and all beings begin.

Native Healers

I duck into the sweat lodge and take my place across from my lifemate, our tribe's medicine man. Knowing our medicine works strongly together, we plan to journey on behalf of a woman in the village who has lost her way. We begin our meditation with deep gratitude as we unfold into the great mystery.

Jolted, I find myself standing alone outside the sweat lodge in another time, on a snaking, smooth path in the mountains where the buffalo cross. Huge other-beasts now barrel down the pathway. One of them crashes through my energy body and shakes my sight from me. I fall, trembling with the loss of everything familiar.

I sense a witness bending over me with an understanding of the times in which we stand. This self is here interpreting what these speeding energies are and explaining what happened to the paths of the buffalo.

Firmly, this energetic other-self takes my hand and arm and leads me to the edge of the high path we stand on, down into a valley where I smell the birch and ash that rise around us. I put my hands out to feel the bark and confirm their treeness. I sense the rustle of a marmot sunning itself on warm rocks. Listening, I hear squirrels above us and the scratchy screams of a hawk, and I count the beats of wings as they uplift on the air. I am led to a creek swirling past us at the bottom of the valley, where I wash away the fear shrouding my eyes.

I see again and dimensions shift.

Returning to the sweat lodge, I remember the trees surrounding me in the future are the granddaughters of trees yet to be planted by this woman on whose behalf we journey.

As my native self again, I tell the shaman this experience.

After tracking what we need from our journeys and cooling down from the sweat, we end up beautifully entwined together on the furs inside our tipi, knowing children and grandchildren will grow in the shade of a great forest whose seeds have yet to be sown.

Seeds

Plant seeds of hope
in unfiltered clouds,
so in their natural growing
they might rain
upon the earth,

to nourish
the bright future

to which we are called.

Toss seeds of light
across the magnificent darkness,
so in their native glowing
they might shine
above the earth,

to blaze
into the intense mystery

from which we were called.

4 Connection

We stand inside the ship of the Chaskakuna, hovering gently over the earth. We are not individual, not he nor she, nor is there any division of them or us. We are One.

Knowing Gaia is awake enough to respond to the presence of our warming lights, we celebrate as we prepare for the next part of our journey.

We slip out of the vessel in response to Gaia's attempts to reach us. Moving across her heavens in a languid, angelic dance, intentionally lowering ourselves ever closer to the ground, our orb of lights lands on the earth, and we release ourselves to that first connection with Gaia's physical essence.

Our lights soak into the ground and spread across the globe in as many pieces and directions as we can imagine, spreading out in a grid, a planned pattern of power for Gaia. Some vortices remain in distinct places where the land responds well. The grid covers the new mountain peaks with as much ease as the desert landscapes.

In that first union with Gaia's soil, our energies transfer, and we open ourselves to unfold into all of life. From our perspective, everything lights up.

The stones report that we lost our lives when we unfolded, but it is not so. The early perception of some fragmented stone, which thought it received only a piece of the whole, began a series of thought which created a misaligned perception of separation in this dimension. True to our essence, everything received the whole.

We first flowed into Gaia's body through caves, past darkened recesses, deep into hollow-throated tunnels sinking below the mantle of her skin, totally in peace with our reception and the union of our beings. Earth held herself open to us, welcomed our merging, and as we penetrated even her darkest chasm to slip into the heated core of Gaia, we further transitioned until our energies coalesced.

The liquid fire deep within Gaia's belly began to steam as we connected, and the condensation rose until caught by cavernous roofs overhead. The underground caves held the moisture which soon fell in spherical drops and built up extreme pools of contained water, a new and necessary component for this living planet. These rolling interior waters forced themselves up from Gaia's depths, erupting as geysers. New steam escaped into the air, rising into the sky to create clouds which roamed over the soils to cool the heat from the energies of our convergence.

As waters filled the lowest valleys which were created when the mountains rose, the first breath of color spread upon the globe in a band that lifted over all of us, and we could taste the sweetness of the shades that filled the air.

When the stones turned inward as a valley of witnesses to review what happened, the rocks recognized the continuity of the Chaskakuna, the interconnectivity of the One. The stones remembered the truth and yet, in the way of stones, telling the whole story of the joining of breath and earth in a new way takes a very long time in human terms.

It is enough to know the Chaskakuna descended.

Reaching

This is a good time to stretch if you want.

Go ahead. Move.

Stand up and reach for the stars like the mountains did. You may not touch them, but you will feel better trying.

Take a deep breath now and blow it all the way out by opening your mouth.

That's right. Do it again.

Use your stomach muscles to breathe. Breathing is good. It is one of the first things we learn how to do.

Now make yourself comfortable.

Open yourself to the heartbeat of the waters upon this land. Feel that subtle pulse where you connect to the ground, recognizing within yourself the familiar movement of your own blood.

Join me in this telling.

Remember and let all things come.

Sense the story now, back when the earliest movements were born, when liquid light first flew over the face of the land, still in a space and a place that is before time.

Watch the skies. You should still be able to see the lights.

5 The Waters

Moisture-laden cells spew from beneath the stones of Earth.

Living drops of light carried from the stars mingle with the fires of the earth, their energies coalescing into tributaries of racing brightness. Foggy clouds form and spread over the land in a heavy, even blanket almost as high as the tallest mountains.

Since the first time of the joining, the Chaskakuna lift up from Gaia as dampness above the land. They rise heavy with condensation, pregnant with life. The clouds span the globe while full drops of clear liquid saturate the air before arriving on the ground. They fall in full color.

As these first drops of water are delivered to the earth, they splatter over the patterned lines imprinted when the Chaskakuna brought their brighter lights to the land. The secure bands of patterned light allow the moisture through and serve to attract only that which offers nourishment to Gaia. The woven energies provide power for the planet as she grows. This is the first test since their gifting. Periodically, the breath of the same wind stirs the clouds, and the power holds.

The land stands still while stones feel a wetness run down their faces, as boulders are tickled by running rivulets, and mountains dip their toes into pools of drops gathering into lakes at their feet. Rivers form in valleys and stones curve into massive tents of sand, swept soft by the rushing fluid.

Slashing pellets of ice daggers along exposed heights quicken the formation of bandages of frozen water as rain dashes against the highest mountains. The cutting is deep. In freezing altitudes, the earliest layers of glaciers are set in place. Thick bindings quicken over a tundra that soon covers parts of Gaia protecting her from the abuse of the crackling water hurtling at her from these new elements. A recognition of stewardship develops in this early outward bonding of the frozen breath of water into a protective covering of the land. The dirt retains a hidden warmth that melts the ice a drop each year, holding the balance between liquid and land.

Softer snowfalls appear in the lower elevations, the water changing character to meet the needs of varying altitudes and the rawness of the risen land. Mountain winds blow a steady chill. Deep into fissures cradled by Gaia and held close to her breasts, the icy snows rest. A synchronicity grows between the high lands and the freezing waters, where the distinction between the two disappears as the color of one becomes the color of the other.

Every place upon the earth waits in elegant stillness as the waters find their courses and fill lakes with their moisture. As the liquid falls and the tension beneath the earth's mantle relaxes, a peaceful equilibrium rises between the underground and the sky above. The reflective properties of the fluid begin to be visible in the settling waters.

Images of mountains line the high lakes. Rushes and reeds in damp swamps look up from their roots. New beaches sparkle with quartz chips still swirling in the waves, collapsing on the land as they set their own boundaries amid the dunes.

The ground embraces the promise of the waters in their various forms as moisture holds a mirror to the stars at night, shining back the lights of the Chaskakuna, still quite aware of the brightness, still in wonder, and grateful for the joining of energies to co-create and clothe the earth.

The waters hold an awareness of Being in their depths. They herald life from the center of each snowflake and each solitary drop of rain.

The primary river, the Madre de Dios, snakes her way around the globe, glowing from within as her very cells reflect the sky-lights of the mother ships and brightest stars along the Milky Way. The water's capacity to reflect is what gives it greater knowledge. Spiraling and turning around the earth, the deepest waters remain silent, pondering what they learn, flowing with the secrets of what they sense and all they breathe.

Glacial Streams

I gasp with cold
as my bare feet slip into frigid waters
of an eroded stream bed
twisting down the glacier.

My feet numb on smooth stream rocks,
while my exposed arms open for a blessing
from the healer with her braided grasses.

I am washed by these waters
that drink me as I stand in them,
my naked soul vibrating in the thin air
of our elevation.

I climb out
as I have scrambled through tunnels,
slipped out of the birth canal,
and risen from the dead or something like it
after hiking miles of mountains,
wet skin turning to the warmth of the lifted sun
and the offered flame.

Later, I sit at a rivulet of a sister mountain,
though this time I taste her,
swallowing the moving waters
to complete the exchange of our energies,
in mutual reciprocity.

Upon the Freezing Lagoon

Sunlight draws chromosomal designs upon waves rippling under frozen sheets in the mountain lake, turning both forms of water into terraced patterns as I watch. Two characterizations of this one element are bridged by cells of light floating between the fluid, the brightness reflecting upon the land to include me in the mystery.

A bubble floats opposite the current and rises to evaporate into the moment.

The lagoon waters freeze at my feet and cleanse the ground holding them while I observe the still point of rippling waves at rest in their valleys. Curled wavelets crest with an expectation, a breath-holding moment, before they yield to the pull of gravity, ever connected to the water of their greater source.

Full of life and movement, the current conveys electric charges of intent before the energy of a bird divides its movement. Separated, the liquid realigns and then comes together to lift the bird and food free of the lagoon in a single synergistic redemptive exhale.

6 Dreaming Beside You

With the lucidity of one falling asleep, I feel my body disappear as the space we share encourages the dissipation of all thought of separation, sweeping us into a single pulsing thread of congruity. I dream of falling to Earth with our souls wrapped in the calm singularity of an exhale. I join with the land of Earth as we ground deeply into soil rising to catch the hope and the light of our becoming.

When we surface, like dolphins delighting in the freedom of the ocean, we touch, cavort, and leap into the sky only to fall back again, laughing within the spray of energetic colors splashing across the heavens, rolling across the ground. We surface less and less, and then further apart, our concepts of time and space distorting with the focus of our joining with Earth and the formative transitioning Gaia experiences while rapid changes ensue after our combining.

Each time our patterns of energy cross closely enough to brush the edges of recognition, the seas holding us tremble with the intensity of truth for our reunions, and our Soul is replenished and reborn. Stars ring in the heavens as we meet. Excited streaks of possibilities infuse with the urge to remember, to know our existence together.

This dream is so lucid.

I sense a difference in the next cycle of time, though for now, we both remember—our arrivals, our lives—and see with a singular focus the power of energy patterns shining across the globe. We pass closely in this cycle of time, striking a chord of conjoined memories that vibrates to the core of our existence. But remembering comes late.

I wake up first, feeling for the warmth of your skin under the hides, seeking assurance of connection in a time and space I am only beginning to shift into.

Ah, there you are.

A touchstone, I reach out to hold you until such time as you, too, disappear into a dream that has not yet happened.

Listen.

Wait.

Breath

Candlelights flame around me in small flickering starts, like stars upon the plains of heaven, the random pulsating brightness almost loud enough to hear as they encircle me while I sit in lotus position upon the ground, intent on holding myself open to the light.

You approach me while your cloak of ancient colors flows from your shoulders, the deep hues vibrating an iridescent glow so rich I cannot watch, though I know you kneel before me.

You reach for my head and tilt my face toward yours as you bend in close to cover my lips with your mouth, and you breathe into me.

I breathe your breath and begin to see, to sense, to slip away from individuation into a place of singular darkness, more alive in ways unknown than before the inhale of that breath.

Now the candles I sense are others also alight with this knowledge, this breath of life, and I begin to understand their silent language.

I rise into you, and we stand so close we fade into each other. When I next open my eyes, I no longer see you but I see through your eyes, feel as your body moves, think coherent and exact thoughts as you think them.

With another breath, I am apart again, immediately pondering the singularity, affirming the unexpected. Aware of these gifts, we begin to travel together as Life-Givers and Bearers of Light.

We are the People of the Stars, in bipedal form, learning of love and light upon the belly of the great She-land of waters.

Together

One on one,
one by one,
two become
that singularity
breathing in, breathing out
a single heartbeat,
wholly visible.

Live with daily gratitude
hoping to grow thanks
in every minute,
awake, aware,
standing
with remembrance
when

one on one,
one by one,
two become
that singularity
breathing in, breathing out
closer than breath,
held between the beats
of the heart.

A Shift in Perception

Journeying to the underworld, I seek to talk with its Lord of Life and Death.

Descending, leaving behind in underground waters all physical concerns, I feel the press of stones against my energetic back as I recline for a moment in a buried river. Allowing the strength of the water to carry me through deeper layers of sand and stone, I stay in the flow until the water empties me into a crystalline lake. A path leading to a garden rises away from where I step out of the water. Walking beyond the healthy plants, I acknowledge the welcoming trees along the outskirts of the grassy meadow. I head for the boulders in the center.

Calling for the Lord of this inner landscape, I walk toward the stones. I realize I am to climb to the top of this pile of boulders. Circling around the base to the back of the rocks, my gaze widens in alarm. I stand at the bottom of a stone pyramid.

I gaze toward the top of this enormous structure and see a zig-zagging path set in the stone to allow travel from the bottom to the uppermost parts. Doubts begin to form. Quizzical, I remember the other side of this pyramid looked like a pile of boulders. I dart back to where I started and find boulders standing there again.

Immediately, I choose to hold this perspective and quickly climb the rocks.

At the flat top of the stones, I stand and hear God's voice calmly telling me to step off of the rocks.

I do not want to believe it.

The voice affirms what I sense: more than just a word of direction, I am commanded to step off the stones. But I do not want to.

And that is when I realize I am afraid. Alone at the top of the mesa, I recognize my lack of trust in Spirit to hold me and keep me safe while I step off a 20-foot high stack of boulders in a dimension that is pure energy.

Reasoning with myself, I argue that if I do not have faith in the Divine when given a small command such as this, what can I rely on, and how can God count on me? Indecision makes my palms clammy, and blood pounds in my ears.

With tears of surrender hot in my eyes, I shift my perspective to one of gratitude and dependence upon my Creator. With images of unseen energetic ley lines rippling in front of and around me, I step off into space.

At once, I stand in the air without appearing to stand on anything solid.

My experience is the same as when I first saw the pyramid versus climbing the boulders: my perception holds me back or encourages me to move forward. Knowing I can make a shift in my inner landscape to allow myself to move into greater possibilities changes the whole picture. While standing on the air, I can travel wherever I want to, at whatever speed I want to travel, to see whomever I want to see.

The miracle overwhelms me.

I am free. My thoughts are what hold me in a false perception that I unwittingly accept as reality.

The difference now is that I am awake.

7 Another Beginning

At the side of a river within the conflux of three banks, I look up from setting leaves afloat. I notice you watching me. We view these small boats as they disappear in greater waves of the river. I feel the light of your smile cross the stream between us.

I join you to sit with our backs to the sun on a gentled grassy beach beside the watercourse. We keep an eye on the sailing boats placed for the hidden people of the streams and waterfronts. Unseen to us, they begin to float the boats, dipping and turning their rudders, swinging out of range of our vision into what could be their future. I stand on tiptoe, holding your shoulder, wanting to see downstream.

With a smile, I ask, "Does the future change for the leaves if I can see them move farther along the river?"

Laughing with you is part of this adventure. Aware of the bending of the grassy fronds rising from the waters, we listen as the river chuckles with us. We have told her a funny joke and her sides can no longer hold in the swells. When she splashes me, I pass the splash on to you.

Ultimately, when you pull me into the stronger water, our hands taste deeper laughter streaming between our fingers as the river sings of speed and varying temperatures. We turn to float on our backs and become large leaves upon the water, supported and moved by this liquid energy. Releasing hands, we slip away from each other, somehow oblivious to the separation. Rejoining downstream carried by the same waves, we reawaken a consciousness that recognizes we were lifted out of sight of each other. Our hands touch, anxious to confirm the solidity expressed, lips caress and our thighs begin to cross each other's, sparking a recognition at once remembered and magnetic in its strength.

Resting while soaking in the water we become drops within the river, sharing a wetness that swirls through us, where we spin into eddies of calming waters basking in sunshine around rising cattail rushes. As our individual lives begin to coalesce, we do what we can to participate in this experience by remaining aware of creation. We launch our thoughts with vibrant memories upon the river of life and set them afloat into the future, releasing them to the unknown.

By the time we rise out of the water, we each agree to set aside remembering we were once dry. We agree to set aside for now, our remembered moments of laughter; to even leave behind the shared thoughts of the hidden people on the leaves upstream, in order that we might grow in new and unpredicted directions.

Embedded in the sand, our footprints and fingerholds soon fill with water and blowing seeds.

We rise from the river, each of us aware of the other, and each taking time to talk to tree and grass seedlings settling in our wake before we leave the beach behind. Our paths diverge.

I stop once, feeling an intense need to remember something. I sense a familiar vibration pulling me to return to the river.

As the notion passes, the trail ahead of me beckons with an unconscious sweetness that lulls me to sleep as I move away from the river. Maybe someday, I will return to these banks. Maybe not.

Today, I walk into the captivating stillness that floats in the heat above this ground, wondering at the mysteries of this land, unaware my skin already pinks from the heat of the shining light.

We each move forward to learn new lessons, not knowing we left any behind.

Flowing

Breathe in from your diaphragm, that large muscle across your belly, feeling your back relax with your next exhale.

Close your eyes.

Be present with your feelings.

Where do you see yourself now? Are you setting leaves upon rivers or out in a part of the river chased by laughter?

Are you leaving a piece of yourself without honoring the forgetfulness?

Feel where you are: notice temperature, stone, waters.

Taste where you are: embrace dampness, freshness, sweet fluids.

Hear where you are: accept heartbeats, insect chirps, splashes.

With your inner eyes open, see yourself: whole, peaceful, hands open.

Smell where you are: intense river scents, wet sand drying, growing river weeds.

Recognize you may be moving through several stages all at once. Express only gratitude.

Be aware of the flow of the river.

Recognize you walk on the same ground holding the rivers. Be at peace with the recognition of connectedness. Where the water flows, the ground supports her. Where they touch, they know their energy as the same. They exist in a permanent supporting embrace.

Stretch your senses. Know the feeling where you are. Love with them.

See yourself from the perspective of a calm eddy in the river, and watch as you flow with the land.

Radiate your sense of self with each faculty at peak awareness.

Be whole.

Be present.

Be seen.

Fissures

The water of my tears
descends into the crevices in my soul,
eroding foundations of walls
once carefully constructed.

The warm liquid
softens scarred wounds,
aiding in the smoothing
of that which was bound
but is now released
as I relearn and claim
knowledge of my purpose.

No longer caged by anxiety,
I breathe deeply,
and when the cool light of day
spills upon my naked soul,
instead of shivering
I begin to shine.

8 Inner Lights

Gathering the energies associated with each of our medicines, I face the shaman in outward silence, as we match our demeanor and begin to breathe together.

Our preparation is fast, but thorough.

Bending our heads together, forehead to forehead, and sharing personal energies in a rite of transmission, we linger together in silence as new vistas open and spread around us in recognition of our ancient connection.

The transmissions complete, we each reach up and grasp a handful of starlight, pausing as we place this light in the other's heart.

Eyes open, we know what to do.

Turning to stand back-to-back, arms fully extend along each other's arms, palms touch, and our heads tilt skyward. Calling on the depths of our combined medicine, vibrations shift.

A vortex opens. Spiraling arms of the galaxy sweep around us.

Tranquility settles in the center.

The portal is open.

Together, we glow.

Gaia's Fire

Fire is not a gift from the gods.

Fire is a gift from the Mother.

Gaia brought nested light-coals with her when she first chose to awaken this organic planet. Her heat recalls an inner journey spent with the sun before she settled in to grow her beloved colors, flavors, scents and sounds. She shares her passion for life with all she is.

As she contemplates wonder, wonder grows. The smallest stones learn this from Gaia when she teaches differing vibrations of energy, how to sense a shift, to anticipate an absence, to roll before heavy winds, how to bend without breaking, or to cool without snapping.

When she first unwrapped the smoking ligaments of light, their deeply magnetic resonance held them tightly together in her core. When she expanded with the joining of the Chaskakuna, Gaia chose some wild fibers of that inner center and freed them, releasing them as seeds of fire to roam the electric grids encircling the globe. Some of those seeds ripen and fly loose as sky-blown lightning to periodically explode across the earth in attempts to reconnect with the core. Various pieces return when bolts of light shock into the ground and pierce the elements through which they travel, seeking center, seeking refuge, finding connection, finding home. Everything resonates with the light and allows passage.

Earth anticipated our arrival. She prepared her nest for the first-born of the Chaskakuna.

Gaia is the holder of the First World of our birthing and the co-creator of the next world of our becoming.

Sudden Heat

The old house burned at midnight,
and after dawn, blackened remains
still drop from trees, blow against my house's brick,
slip from rooftops, slap into the ground,
barely holding shape until touched
to disintegrate into that which is
unrecognizable, as if finally
able to release the carried images
burned out of existence.

Black oak leaves checker my lawn
with grimy bits of roofing and siding
which crumple when lifted as they crash into ash
besmirching my view of Fall's
oranges, reds, and russets.

I see the trail where pieces
flew away from flames,
lifting, though briefly, into outstretched arms
of the neighboring oaks, only to slip
as charcoaled remnants,
through branches of the living trees
capable of holding the dead only a moment,
lest the friction from the release of life
be passed quickly, scorching their own leaves.

Rising over charred cinders,
tall grasses hold the residue
amid the dewdrops of morning
glistening through the shadowed shells
of broken leaves.

It was a wet spring,
a dry summer,
and the promises of fall
include sparks of sudden heat.

Elders at the Edge of the Fire

Traveling where the energy takes me, I grow small and zip to a fire somewhere in the North American foothills.

The women catch my eye as they circle-dance, but that is not what intrigues me. The Native Grandmothers see me looking out from the edge of the fire and whistle for me to fly over to them.

One crone wants me to flutter to her outstretched finger. Trusting my instincts and passing by this woman, I flit over to Oldest Grandmother who sits farthest from the fire.

Blind in one eye, this woman invites me to perch on her shoulder as Hummingbird, where we whisper truths to each other.

Then we look in each other's eyes, left eye to right eye.

I view the birth of a galaxy in her depths before noticing loose threads in her awareness. With an almost imperceptible nod of assent, I help her release what she wants to sever, so nothing remains to hold her back.

Watching, I hear stars from the Milky Way as they move in her soul.

She is bright, and we share a sense of trust. Though our languages differ, our hearts understand.

Dark Leaves Under the Moon

Dark leaves slip before me
on blackened asphalt
where shadows of red oak tremble
under the light of the stars,
and the road I am on begins to ripple
like a rug shoved against the curb.

I hesitate before taking my next step,
certain of nothing more than
the movement of the street
as I stand still in the shifting penumbra,
weighing risks between the waving pitch
and the island of pavement.

Carefully, I tiptoe on silvered spaces
illumined by the veiled stars,
as if stepping onto their argent orbs
flickering between the leaves.

I climb, rising above
dimensioned shadows
on a journey that takes me
to the burnished fullness
of the Moon.

Stepping onto loose ash,
dust balloons around my form
as I push off, weightless,

angling toward an inner cavern
where waits the welcome
of an ancient spirit.

I call her Grandmother,
she who calls me home.

9 Wandering

Don't think.

Just sit there for a moment.

When was the last time you let your mind wander? Invest in the in-between place where you suspend belief.

Are you breathing? Watch for the depth of the next breath.

Pull in air from the belly. This keeps the color and direction in your life as you learn to paint these pictures with brilliant pigments.

Can you see the lights? Not just in the stars.

Look around you. They are in the fabric of everything that is.

Now close your eyes.

Don't think.

Listen from within, from that place of your breath.

Be present to all your senses.

Be alive!

Born of the Joining with Fire

We are born in the waters of the fire beneath the stone. We grow in awareness and will never be the same. The heat of the water is not considered a temperature; it just is. Hot. Passionate.

The dirt, the air, the fire, and the water that are born of the Joining do not have any distinct names. Changes upon us are great and fast. Drops of falling water expand and contract our membranes as we grow beside each other.

We are aware.

We move, and we breathe together.

With the quickening, we gather other cells around us. We differentiate our purposes and work together to grow new membranes, new bodies, new senses. More cells gather until a rush of exotic wind brushes across the height, the width and the breadth of Gaia with a low musical toning.

The pitch rises.

From the colors of the grasses as we green upon the earth, animated hues sweep across the globe in a riotous wave of welcome.

Painted in effervescent shades across the earth, we stretch into new shapes and change our habitat. We associate. We grow identities.

Greeted by land and liquid, we support each other, feeding in the air and under the ground. In return, we give to each what is needed for life to breathe upon this planet. We grow closer in these new embodied dimensions.

We begin by nourishing our souls.

Consumed

I sit across from the Angel of Life. This Being places an ember from a ceremonial fire in each of my hands.

Vibrating at a level I do not comprehend, I sit with my fingers cupping live coals that burn against my palms. The ligaments of my body expand with steam as I feel myself falling into flames.

I am consumed.

White bones lie talking amid orange and red embers. Hitherto undisclosed images lift off the length of the bones, interior messages of mathematical sequences, tattooed numbers exposed in the heat appearing darker than the ash surrounding them, rising and fading as the fire dims, fragments cool, and coals gray into stillness.

A slight wind stirs.

The question is asked, "What is left?"

Surprised, I answer, "I am."

The All-Flaring

I listen to the flames
of the fire in Odin's throne room,
hearing the beginning sounds of day
coalesce into life as four raven wings
strike into a new rising
as they fly back into
the shadows of night,
chasing bits of story upon the wind.

In my musing, I am blind
to flying embers from the fire,
until one spark
strikes the back of my hand,
the bite of hot coal
a searing yet passionate embrace,
at once immediate
and permanent.

Intense light settles within my flesh,
the head of this fiery comet
charging straight through my soul,
across the heavens like a fireball,
shooting through a celebration of remembrance,
where the veils holding memory
lift away from the stars
framing their existence,
so nothing is hidden
from the eyes of those who seek.

Burning, I let the comet arc
away from my heart
and find its way home
to yours.

10 Breathing

Hold your breath.
Close your eyes.
Be aware of your senses.
What are you smelling? What are you seeing? What are you hearing? What do you feel?
Exhale. Inhale.
Hold that breath, too. Longer. There.
Do you feel that inner beat?
Can you sense the deep tones of color and ripening sound that sink toward the earth? That rise from her being?
Breathe normally and stretch your senses. Follow that beat as far as you can into the depths of the ground. Remain aware of yourself.
Journey to listen, feel, smell.
One more time, take a deep breath. Exhale.
Is anything different?
Rise then, returning along that same thread, back to the beat you started from upon this earth. The sound, the scent, the touch are yours.
Remember.
You are fully present.

Finding Place

A hawk cry screaming in the background of the night echoes in my dream.

In that semi-lucid place between worlds, as the shaman's woman, I answer the call and rise from beneath the warming robes. Walking over sleeping bodies, I push the skin flaps up, and slide out of the tipi. I stand under the sky.

Here, it is clear. I am meant to be a shooting star. I am meant to cross the skies of others' lives, arcing a trail of light that is neither wide nor narrow, but which others can see should they choose to follow. This that I am, a woman of prairie grasses, comes from those stars, reverberates with an energy that cannot be named but can be felt.

Tonight is a time for running the stars. Like celebrations and ceremonies for the running of the buffalo herds, this quiet darkness holds a time of freedom to dance and slip away with the lights.

Slowly creating a wide circle, my silent feet step upon the ground that meets me, heel–toe, heel–toe, flat foot, flat foot, repatterning the position of the stars that move inside.

The pursuit of the shining brings a joyful comfort.

The magnetic draw of the tumbling stars sings my body frequencies higher, releases my soul into a wild dance with the light of the moon as it, too, stirs in the fluid that is night.

Sensual reflections from the rays of the moon dip into the ethers of existence.

I circle again, swaying with deliberate precision, my feet repeating, repeating a new birthing pattern, and soon I am lifted and set down upon the earth in a new place, in a new way, with a new understanding of self, others, and my place in life on the mothering planet.

As I slow, my hands reach out. I am aware you are present, watching from inside the tent.

I return to the grounding of the hides, embodying an inner light, already pregnant with brightness.

Unfettered, I

let go,
trusting the Creator exists
in all I cannot see.

I open wings.

Releasing a clawed hold
on branching strands of silver
whose shadows
are of my own creation,

I rely upon the Source
blowing me
beyond the nest.

I lean into the Unknown
where surely,
as I no longer stand,

I fly

Somewhere, Searching

Traveling this evening within the landscape of the mountainous Andes, I am to locate my teacher, a Peruvian paqo or healer, I met in a meditative journey. I trust my tracking instincts, and yet I move up the rocky trail feeling an anxious hesitation.

Hiking around boulders in this crisp and arid land, I crest a foothill under the timeless gaze of the great mountain lords and hear a piper echoing music from the hillside. I follow playful notes which float knee-high across the plains in waves of colored light. I pursue them as they lead, and so I notice in the distance an open ruin where three sides of a stone wall enclosure remain standing. There is someone sitting cross-legged inside the fragmented remains, so I approach in silence not wanting to disrupt his meditation.

The paqo for whom I search appears with his flute, leaping into the center of the incomplete room, taking my full attention.

We circle across from each other, this native healer and I, neither of us stopping our circuitous route until I realize the movement changes nothing.

When I acknowledge I circle because I am not sure I belong, my movement stops. Looking more closely, I recognize the seated figure as a close friend, and I do not want to intrude.

Moving behind the seated figure, I kneel close to him within that place of ancient stones. Inside that sacred space, he reaches behind him with one hand and pulls my thigh close to his back. I rest vibrating hands on his shoulders, and we merge into a single awareness, alive in a totally different place and time.

Reality folds.

I stay present enough to realize we are on a star in a galaxy with multitudes of stars moving around us where I hear lights talking across the universe as stars shoot past, and they understand me as well. Sending thoughts of love, kindness, health and peace to them, they, in turn, surround us with a profound sense of joy and acceptance.

This is the place of non-duality, the advaita. This is that place of being before the division of breath.

I am aware that we are the core of the star itself. We are that which shines.

The paqo holds that bridge of space with us, and three of us return to the ruins on the mountainside.

As I recall my physical presence again, I breathe intently to integrate back into the present where my hands gravitate to the ground. Held by the earth, I breathe in and out, wondering about reality and what matters.

What really matters?

11 Grounding

It is time to step outside.

Yes, outside your home.

The time of day does not matter. Afternoon, evening. Deepest night. Maybe it is tomorrow morning, but it is time for you to do this.

The weather is not bothered that you go out into it. The ground does not shift its position according to when you do this.

But you will know if you skip this step. Your body will know.

Prepare yourself. Wear that new scarf or old jacket. Step into those slippers or loose shorts or walk out bare-chested. No one cares what you wear. Only your skin will know.

Move outside now.

Use your inner eyes and find the place outside where you connect to the ground.

Yes. This is the spot.

You do not need to wander over to that other place. Or that one, either.

Be content with your choice, for it is the right place. There is no other space for you than this one.

Now lie belly-down upon the earth.

Yes, all the way down.

Pull up your shirt, open your sweater, or unzip your jacket. Do whatever you need to do to lean your belly directly against the ground.

Expose your skin to the Mother's.

Face down, breathe in gently. Smell the greening under the frosted layers of leaves. Feel the grainy sleet as it pelts against your back where you connect to the earth. Listen to the pound of the surf that rises from the sand through your belly. Taste the richness rampant in the patience of the Earth's colored skin.

Release the tension inside you. Let it go into the ground.

Give gratitude to Earth for the holding. Give thanks for the learning.

Open your inner eyes. Allow yourself to be playful and crack open each of your senses. Invite yourself to remember those times that flash by, the lights of other days, the delights of now.

Welcome the magic. Trust from deep within yourself.

Oh, yes! This is the place. Source from here.

Turn over. Notice the sky. Feel the Earth supporting you, just you, at this moment of intense connection.

Rise up when you are ready, and watch the land open her beauty to you. Mirror back the great peace in which you find yourself.

Stand with an open heart.

Shine back joy.

You do not need the book. Set it down after you read these pages. It will be here when you return.

To the Mountains, From a Star

The mountains did not have to greet us. Some of them still think they do not reach us. But they do—energetically, psychically, holistically. We are touched as they are touched. The caresses are mutual.

We change before we leave our portals to descend, for the joining is on many different levels.

When we meet Gaia, the light that is struck in our passage to the skin reforms and reestablishes the power set loose in the patterns upon this planet. With the vibrations free, creative energy folds. Time repeats itself. Especially when there is a witness awake to the crease in the tapestry, we can see the shimmer, we are aware of the repetition.

This is what it feels like, soft and familiar.

Can we be in the same place twice, thinking the same thoughts, breathing the same breaths?

We awaken another level of experience with the ability to see the wrinkle before it is smoothed out.

As we recognize the division breath creates, that initial moment of separation, we cross into stillness and remember our beginning.

The First Grandmother

Earth drops away beneath me as I lift toward the heavens. I land in a different world in a pasture of tall waving grasses filled with llamas, goats, cows and sheep. I wander through this herd of beautiful, healthy animals and hear the steady, rhythmic milking of an animal just ahead of me. I drop down—not wanting to be seen—for I do not really know where I am.

When I first see the back of the woman bent over and milking a small four-legged animal, every fiber in my body cries, "Mother!," and my short legs begin to run toward her. However, I run as a small cat, and my cries come out as "Meow!"

The tall woman hears me and responds with a greeting. A steady squirt of milk reaches my mouth with such delicious richness I stop and smile while I lick it all away. I rub against her legs with love and gratitude, and when she finishes this ancient chore, she picks me up and wipes the remaining milk off my face. I purr even louder against her chest. I am totally content, utterly filled, held, loved and at peace.

The milking done, the woman turns to other obligations, sets me down and I drift away again, into the star-lit heavens.

Taken back to where my journey began, I reflect on my experience, and ask about the place I visited. At once, I remember this is the place of Earliest Beginnings, the home of the Mother of Grandmothers, the Forever One from whom all love pours.

Tears fill my eyes that I did not speak to Her, the Mother of Creation, and give her thanks for my life. Only then do I realize I did speak in terms of love. She knew me as I rubbed against her legs and cried out a call of recognition to which she responded with immediate nourishment. We shared a moment of love as I purred against her chest, and I still feel that deep resonance within my bones.

I journeyed to a place not so very far away. I journeyed to the cusco, that center we all hold within ourselves: a place of love and deepest peace with that inner calm which is the setting in which we know the voice of God.

The Mother had other children to feed, and I know she sang out to one of them as I was leaving. Her voice sounded as if it were of water rippling through air, like a breathless, "Om, Gaia."

Tomorrow, Undreamed

There are few remaining who sing the stars
to lift the moon above the earth.

But shamans listen to the beat
of the heart within the mountains,

knowing they live for a time
until the planet's greatest exhale

catapults a few pieces of creation
into the next world.

If you, too, can listen for the pulsing
of the moon as it crests the earth,

then perhaps you will learn
of what these healers sing

and tomorrow may be birthed
into the present of which you dream.

12 Climbing at the Center

After the fading of the discordant tones of a midnight train, Grandmother comes to my bedside. I see a gossamer thread draped from her weavings and grasp the yarn to climb toward her.

Climbing as spider, as she who weaves the web of original threads upon which the layers of the world are stretched, I move in fluid silence. My webs are those lucid dreams upon which the worlds of the present are woven.

Resting my dreams upon the lights stretching around Gaia, I leap between layers without wrinkling the fabric. Grandmother invites me to spin, to crochet, weave, and knit with spindly-legged tools that clack in rhythms echoing across the central web after the train passes.

Evenly spaced, hypnotically balanced in sound and sight, the creating never stops. Like gigantic patterned vapors repeating themselves in an otherwise barren sky, I knit threads which whip into a knotted cable of sweatered clouds. I am called to spin, to knit, to weave and create themed cloud banks to store for changes in weather. When I rest, I turn to the arms of the trees around me, scramble my shadow up along a rising bole and relax my legs as if to branch out against the sky. My body stretches, indivisible from the trunk and limbs. In a seemingly collective concert, I fall to Earth in my dreams and waken with only four limbs and a mass of yarn stretched around my bed.

Floored

Come, join me.

Sit cross-legged, if you can, in a semi-lotus position, right there.

Face me. That's it.

Make your legs comfortable. Keep your back straight. You may sit on the cushion if you need to.

Our knees touch, gentled into this position, close and supportive. We lend strength to one another in thought.

Breathe with me, long exhales that empty our lungs. And now another breath, relaxing into a synchronized pattern at once recognized and remembered, though the rhythms feel new to these forms we embody.

One more breath together to feel the solidarity of the land supporting us and the rise of the heavens above us.

Feel the shift in the air as we grow in height, stretching into the light that lifts from us as if we are the very heart of the tallest redwoods. Sense our growth into this dear earth, roots vining around crevices and buried boulders, tucking thoughts into the rich, velvet darkness of the soil.

Open your eyes and look at me, my friend. Let me gaze into your depths at the same time, sharing with you what lies behind the dark irises of my eyes.

Lift your hands before you as I lift mine before me.

Turn your palms toward me as I turn mine toward you. Let them touch.

Close your eyes. I close mine.

Lean into my hands as I lean into yours.

And, if your hands are not stopped by my hands, nor my hands by yours, let us continue to lean into each other until that moment we again breathe together—though this time we breathe as one, not because we are aware of being together, but because as we inhale now, we are no longer separate. There is no awareness of being together because we no longer have an awareness of being distinct or disconnected from anything or anyone. We remember.

In time, let us uncross our energy.

I see you with different vision. I see through your eyes, with you. We recognize and know that what we are is no less beautiful than the sight before us.

Rise with me as you are able, when you are ready, feeling the vibration of your soul in this unlimited time and place. The soft holding in this space leads to a great inner grounding, and in silence, I invite you to step outside where our inner sense of support expands.

Offer that sensuous feeling of communion to the skies where the intricate sine waves of our crossed signatures turn to stardust filtering through the layers of the universe.

We lift our hands between us, and they touch.

I know you feel it. I feel it. They touch.

As in the beginning, our very hearts touched.

Unraveling

She stands in the backyard as dogs
unravel the leftover grass runners
tenaciously hugging the ground
inside the wooden fence,
even after last summer's drought.

Mists lift away from the hot mug
of lemon tincture held cupped in her hands
as she blows steam into the hole
of a newly-webbed moon.

She watches this full light rise
through spider-legged branches
of oak and sweet gum and fig
whose curves now straddle the sky
after the spinning is complete.

As these arachnid branches
gracefully bend away from her
in chilling winds that prickle
tiny hairs above her neck,
the spindly creatures gently step
out of the trees,
and onto the stars.

Strands

As the spider web cupped between purple asters like a crystalline goblet set down among the grasses, I catch sunlight and stardust to quench the thirst of souls.

My strands connect to yours, not side by side on this divergent path, but as if we are mirrors, turned toward each other, where one is seen just above the other, hovering a dimension apart, ever feeling each other but never touching.

I sense color through the fibrous threads elongating around me where I am inundated with vibrations. Serpentine frequencies slide themselves through me.

One sudden thrust of wind from underneath me inverts my concave webbing, and I lose my hold on the seedhead. Floating away with a single cord lifting my body higher and farther than I ever thought possible, I allow myself to go.

This silver-fine thread of morning luminescence, the invisible sticky filament of evening, lifts me into the heavens where I catch a shifting thunderhead. This thread soon drops, and I move from one dense cloud to another, a broken web in the sky between roiling masses of moisture.

The wind, the rain, and the sun drip me back to the ground where I disappear into the web around the earth. Heavy with sunlight, drenched in starlight, awake with self-awareness, I land. I-land. Island.

Did I mention transformed?

Movement in the River

I can't believe I tripped.

I bent to watch the moon's shadow deepen in long eddies along the river bank and when I rose and turned, my toes lost their grip on the stone. Arms flailing, I grabbed the nearest branch that reached out to catch me.

With detached clarity, I watched the slow motion glide of my fall and recovery. The grasp of the tree was the only evidence I needed as I swung into the water where my naked legs disappeared into the flow of creation. As I suspected, this is the original place: the place I landed when I fell from the stars.

The river looks wet yet feels dry. When I scan its pulsing depths, I see wind and stone as ashen shadows bereft of shape or color, but electric with an energy I sense before I see.

This remains an early place of crossing, where trees branch their roots down into the River of Life and those roots branch back to this Earth.

Once, we gathered on this shore. I see faded imprints from our first footholds and finger holes pushed into the sand where we rose from deeper levels of experience some recall as an earlier world. I remember the impossibility of breathing deeply until we reached this level.

My chest rises and my lungs expand with the recollection. The sweetness of the Ruh permeates my being, and I unfold in this place.

Settling beside the river, I remember arriving here at this conflux of flowing streams where an odd number of watersides rise. I specifically remember two of us: one who is being reborn (that would be me), and you, just ahead of me. The trees were smaller then. Our paths diverged.

I see a future allowing us to run across another meadowed brightness, a freshly-healed land, hand-in-hand above a ground bright with joy. We share our beginnings in the stars, sliding the skies with the humming of the sounds of Light, transporting peace in rivers of vibration.

But I am not there yet.

I tripped, and the offered branch helped me catch myself. Now, looking in the river, I see the colorless energy.

Sorrowed, I cannot enter that fluid with full release to the next level until I know the light as mine. Something in my story remains to be told.

However, I am aware you slipped through the river and left a note in the shadowed edges of the moon. Was it you who alerted the tree to catch me before I fell?

Now I kneel at the river searching her depths, aware I am watched, remembering another time when I was also watched, like this.

Searching, I bend again to look for the beginning of the moonlight that cast its shadow on my feet and hooked onto my toes. I yearn for the question my life answers, knowing the two were birthed as one.

This ashen River of Creation between worlds holds many questions, while my ears tingle with vibrations. I hear, but dimly distinguish the sounds.

Ah, Mother of God. My feet tripped on a stone. That is one perspective.

What if the stone moved of itself, and my feet were stable?

What if the tree wants communion and desires not only to reach out and catch me, but to communicate what it knows I seek?

What must I become to be ready to venture into a place I both recall and forget?

What must I do to trust that which I do not yet know or remember?

13 A Collective

We become stronger as the waves of grasses and bush, trees and brush rise from the globe and reach toward light. The brightness of the sun commands our attention, pulling our bodies to follow its crossing. When our shadows merge into the evening light, we expand into the softer appeal of the night sky. The depth of this darkness punctuated with starlight sends us messages the tallest yucca trees elect to decode.

We learn and call into our present forms more information from the places of light, those farthest spaces of being.

Communities remaining connected, we divide. We elongate our senses of self and move as undulating invertebrates, rising and lowering ourselves as larger units upon the earth and in the seas.

Gaia sounds out names like "butterfly," "bee," "stingray," and "coral"–new notes to vibrate along the grid stretching around her skin. We grow identities around ourselves of the simple purposes of our lives.

We mulch the soil into optimal growth. We spread soft roots within the waters of the lakes.

Dividing ourselves, we multiply.

Gaia sings us into her being, one membrane at a time, and we touch each other in our communities, aware our growth is intertwined with those we feel and those they touch, and those even more removed. We flow along this river of silence, slipping into that spiraling depth until we know more and climb out the underside into a new world inviting us to breathe deeply.

As we exhale, we vibrate.

We hum and sing. We have heart.

The new music of our being rises in connection with All That Is, attracting orchestral sounds upon the wind as wings beat a soft yet steady rhythm.

Our vibration increases, and once again we rise into new growth.

Connecting

Are you sitting? You might want to recline.
Now, breathe deeply. Breathe into your womb, that belly of creation.
Breathe a strong breath—in and out.
Relax your lips and nostrils, and expand your awareness from this place.
Take a soft, profound breath.
Pull in the scents of your body, the sense of your being, and allow the fluidity of your inhale to calm the furthest recesses of the pool of wisdom holding your name.
Listen and feel that sense of yourself.
Attend to that which moves or rises across your vision but attach no meaning. Follow the colors, the numbers, the images or letters that shift in this place. If you do not understand an image, ask for clarity.
Wait.
Offer gratitude.
Feel the freedom from where your breath sources. Acknowledge the beginning of this Ruach of life, this one breath, one spirit.
When you rise, touch another and while hugging, be hugged.
Feel the connection that exists as you exhale together.
Be in this sensitive place of connection.
Let us share our breathing and disappear.

Rock Still

I sit on an ancient ledge carved into a rocky outcrop and slip into silence gazing into the branches of the eucalyptus forest spread around me. Gifting a three-leafed k'intu of coca leaves to the huge block of stone holding me, I relax to watch the leaves flutter to rest in a bowl of shadows too deep for my hands to reach the bottom. Acknowledging the stillness of the stone, I get away, take time to go within.

Mythically climbing down stone steps carved into the interior of the boulder, I notice the lack of exterior light. I expand my awareness into the circumference of the rock, feeling it as my own skin. While I rest my body in the light of the sun, my thoughts continue to sink into the abyss of blackness. I connect with breath as my only constant while everything else recedes.

The stone guides me further along to its darkened core. My feet splash in a shallow pool, and I stop at the unexpected change. Detecting a lighter sheen from this small interior pond, I settle into an inner alcove felt along the shore, comfortable in the silence that swells from this place.

The ripples from my movement are gone. New currents form in the inner rock stillness of this stone.

I sense this water serves as the lips of Earth and life ascends from the heart of this place. The water-filled lips are full of story, and I am heartened as I remember I am to transcribe these words connecting our lives, our loves, and our souls.

From an Apprentice

I unfurl as the petals of a lotus flower,
draping over my prayer bundle
like the flower your fingers spread
outlining that colorful corolla,
the meaning of your life
continuing to influence mine.

You flourish in your city like a low-lying flower
whose deep roots hold it secure,
allowing the core of robust colors
to open, scant breaths away from the soil
where healing words settle
as seeds into fresh loam.

I will journey to where your blossoms
hold their faces to the light,
that I may search the tiny flora
for the grace which lines your eyes.

14 Skins for Ceremonies

My hands are steady as I hold the newly-wrapped deer hide stick ready to call in the voice of my drum. The Mothers and I worked on the doeskin over the times of frozen ground. Now with oak leaf growth turning the air yellow in the haze of setting suns, the Grandmothers agree this night's land ceremony should be the first for me to raise the timbre of this vessel of sound.

The drum skin glows a soft cream in the light of the fire, though by day I know her to be white. At the time of the naked moon, I finished stroking brilliant gold rays to one side, allowing some of the lustrous facets to blend over the edge as if melting onto the hoop. Tonight, flashes from this painted star rise into dimensions I usually see in times of deep thought; but with this night's magic, I see the pulsating glow on the skin of the drum before I even touch her hide.

After dancing to the flames of the fires, where my feet pattern shadows from fiery blazes into this hard ground, I ignite the shimmer growing inside my heart. I lift the drum toward the birthing moon. Draped in matching deerskin hide, I absorb with her skin the darkness into which we cast the light we share together in this creation.

When I feel her weight upon my arms, I hold her higher, until the rhythm in my chest matches the beating in my feet, the singing in my arms. Sensing the stick moving of its own accord against the hoop,

I follow its tapping to guide the tip to sound on the virginal center of the skin.

The surreal vibrations cause me to step outside myself.

I lower the drum to where she hovers over my heart. My own observer, I remain aware as the radiance of the star jumps into the night with each beat, seeming not to retain alignment with any sense of space or time. Mesmerized, I watch the pulse of the star through half-lidded eyes, dancing higher as I cross a bridge reaching from the fire to my home in the heavens.

The pounding increases before our cries come together as we stretch ourselves tight against the hoops created for our lives, all the while beating, beating, and stomping new patterns of sound. No longer aware of any association with the ground or the vastness of space, so intertwined are we in the naked, open pounding of the freshness of this drumming, I do not know my voice ever separate from hers.

She sings of ecstasy echoed in my cries of the immortal sounds of love, the twin souls of our measured cadence surging over Earth in tones that at once caress and throb with passion for this newness of living.

This She-land vibrates with the drumming even after I collapse, skin against skin.

In my dream, I hear our combined voices rise from the ground, reverberating against the arcs of inner Earth. I feel their rising and falling in the creation of tonal bridges others climb to revel in this intimacy, this level of expression of the lives we lead.

Upon my waking, the sounds continue as increased colors in my vision where I now see to plant the seeds for tomorrow's corn.

I dance upon these fountains of sound, flutter my breath into their very hues, and lean into each day with gratitude for the beating of my

heart as it stills into one beat with the Mother.
    I am peace.
    I am love.
    Now, during the day, I glow.

No Separation

Stinging blood pulses through my calves as movement reawakens dormant muscles.

I stretch my legs forward into forced stillness along a single bank of the rivers at this confluence. I am alone.

When I place palms against the speckled shore to shift deeper into comfort, I notice three creases on the back of my right thumb imitate lines of strata recorded in the rock.

Shivers of recognition wash over me.

As I watch, my skin ripples and blends with the color of stone until there is no difference. I see no separation, and I wonder am I as much the stone as I am the hand?

All pretention to isolation implodes in the disappearance of difference. I change, and my senses expand exponentially.

Time and space mean nothing.

Life continues in fluid appreciation.

When twilight settles, stars clamor for my attention. Soon I recline on the river's edge.

When the skies stop moving, I watch the heavens shift through varying degrees of lightening grays and yellows until the final image of brightness blinds my physical senses.

Lone stars fade in the ultimate light. Not one piece of creation is isolated while everything stands together.

There is no separation. This is my last thought before I realize I am disconnected, free from hands, breath, body, stone–yet I am aware of my existence.

Then, sensing your presence, I am gone.

The Bright Shining

At three, I am not as tall
as the flowers I stand beside,
and I hold my breath
so I don't grow taller.

But the butterflies find me
and lift me up.

They fly me high and set me down
where I dip my feet in the noisy stream
running rampant among the leaves
of the second-story trees.

My eyes widen as I watch
bright stars bob in this stream,
and I play where I am known
in this place among the heights,
this place among the stars.

When I look for my reflection
in the waters, I cannot see
beyond the bright shining.
I have no sense of separation
living with the known,
the unknown, and the maybe,
outside the inside of my own becoming.

Releasing

Step into the water here, beside me. There is plenty of room. Not too deep.

Now, feel the flow of the stream as it comes toward us.

Be aware of how the bedrock holds you. Notice wind and sky. What do you feel at your back?

Recognize the water—deep, strong, resilient.

Shift your perspective. Sense globally.

Be the liquid in her layers and waves. Ripple in congruence with her movement around the planet. There is no division between your experiences. You are here. You are there.

Standing in the waters, release prayers of gratitude. Ask the water's spirit to replenish its freshness.

We are temporary tenders of these bodies. Barkeeps. Any sense of control is illusory.

Care for your charge. Be form, recalling formlessness.

Watch the observer and notice peace.

Perceive your vibration shifting when we share peace. Not space, that indeterminate distance to be decoded into understandable parts.

Breathe out what you are holding and allow complete release.

Let the movements of the earth and her waters offer you solace, and discard what is not necessary. Drop thought; be wholeness.

Vanish into the absolute Present.

15 First Tree

Before the bark closes around the heart of the first tree, grasses grow thick and pull the dirt around her base to blanket new roots. A thick skirt of fresh earthen scents climbs into the air around her, waiting.

Green grasses become still, pregnant in that moment of quiet expectation when the original thoughts of the tiniest tree begin to move into shape. The core of Tree creates herself simultaneously with an outer coat of bark which hardens in gusts of wind and the brilliance of light. Soon the pattern is established, and she grows in height to spread arms wide, engaged with growing rings.

Tiny branches leaf out. Shadows sweep over grasses that offered the first blessings of soil.

Vines begin to climb Tree's trunk amid blossoms hanging in drowsy succulence, adding to the rich moisture in the air. Sturdy branches sprout, twisting around Tree in a double helix, creating stair steps for more forms of life to rest, build nests in, or climb.

When she grows as close to the clouds as she can possibly grow, Tree does not stop. She leaves the familiar heartwood, the core, the bark, her many rings, bole, and branches, continuing her journey into the sky. When she looks back to Earth far below her, the stimulating freedom of growth keeps her from missing her previous understanding of herself only as Tree.

With gratitude, the transfiguration complete, she rises into another world, taking nothing with her.

Awareness shifts, and she is greeted with joy. Everything is already present.

Fully transformed, Tree begins to move into shape, concurrently covering her core with an outer coat of brightness which swirls in soft winded breaths singing from within a brilliant light.

She grows, singing herself into a matriarchal tree, laden with fruits for sharing. Ripened produce loosens its hold on her branches, releasing from Tree to fall onto a Caretaker's wind. Brilliant bags of seed-stars soon lie tucked into whirling breezes across multiple realms as more trees rise to this place.

A forest of glowing timber breathes with the land, undulating in perfect synchronicity. Swells appear in the dappled shadows under a leafy canopy, layers of sound sorting themselves into a living translucence of gradient light, holding promise of growth.

The voice of the Tree increases in intensity to match the surfeit of chords surrounding her. The music builds, ring upon ring, a vibrating circle around the girth of the planet, extending above and below the Mother Tree where she rises, an arc within the greater circumference.

She stands still and full of Knowledge.

Streaming

Sit on the ground.

Yes, connect to the land.

Take a deep breath in and feel your body heavy and centered into the land as you exhale.

Pull in a belly full of air and release a long gust of wind that blows the dust away from your psyche.

Notice by sight or touch or sound, lines leading to you and away from you, as connecting tunnels or veins of energy of the earth, meeting in you and circling through you.

Fluid streams of light run up your body as water up the roots of Tree rise to the uppermost branches. Excited, notice there is so much more!

Streams of energy move into your hands, your feet, your heart, connecting, circling, encircling, arcing in smaller and then larger spheres of luminescence. Bathed in invigorating color, ecstatic sound, you tingle with an awareness of this moment, awash with waves of beauty singing on the wind.

Flow into the lines of the moving symbol of eternity surrounding you.

Turn with gentled practice around the twists of the Celtic knot.

Breathe into the layers of the moving Nautilus, expanding your sense of presence into new dimensions around you.

Rise into awareness of the beating of the unseen realms sitting with you, those who sense you in their presence, while your connections remain almost unimaginable yet so vibrant.

Open your inner radiance to the endless flowing light.

See the seed of brightness planted which becomes you. Watch your growth into this shifting place of rotating lights.

Your Mother Tree plants you.

I see my Mother Tree planting me.

Each of us grows as part of a planting, turning inward and turning outward, rotations within rotations.

We grow as Trees. Tall, reaching to the light.

Inside, we grow the light as bright pillars, segments of the spheres, arcs of the chords, a flash across the heavens.

Radiate inward.

Be.

Know.

Breathe your light.

That Which Makes Things Visible

Light leans its presence,
smooth and thick like honey,
against the trunk of the oak,
filling cracks where tree bark
furrows in chiseled crevices.

A faint lambency seeps into the tree
and slowly husbands a passage
across the heartwood,
flowing in and out of porous rings
until it travels through the fibrous matter.

This luminescence casts no shadow
ahead of its radiance,
spilling instead a steady, golden luster
beyond what once appeared in form
as tree.

Heart Music

Stepping out into the twilight, feeling into the darkness that floats around me like a soft winter coat, I am wrapped in cottoning layers of stillness and held in the leftover warmth of the evening.

I move toward a quiet tree and begin a soft spoken conversation. I introduce myself; notice the response.

Talking in languages I know, the tree shares the rhythm of its heart song.

I stand rooted beside its radiance as it tunes the music inherent in its being. My hand rests against its trunk. My eyes close to the prana moving between us, so I no longer see the patterns riding the bark. So transparent are we, the mice run by without pause while my hand disappears into the vertical mazes of the rising bole.

Then comes the song, released to the moon, from the heartwood of the towering conifer. The sighing of the music slipping under my fingers flows in counterpoint to the expression of the moonlight.

This is tonight's song. Tomorrow may be different. I simply listen, learning the heart music, picking up the tune that is shared, feeling its rootedness around me.

I discover I am a caretaker of trees in the garden. Holding a bag of seeds, I plant the forest.

Feeling the vibrations of the smallest seeds as they are set out, I scatter them loose into the deep rich soil of the universe, covering them not only with the silence of the damp, but singing them to radiance, to rise into the light of hope that opens all around us, shining from the sun and the reflections of the greater light within us.

As these trees rise to be open light-bearers, so grow the seeds we plant, ready to mirror back that which they see.

I continue to listen in order to circumvent pruning, learning when to let go to allow the pillars to stretch in height and in girth, hearing a deep-toned ringing in the growth.

Encouraging heart-songs, I too, sing my core to brightness, honoring the ground which holds us cradled between Earth and Heaven.

16 Standing

You need to stand.
Come on all the way up.
I will steady you as you rise.
Take my hand.
    Stand with me and know yourself as Tree, a pillar of light stretching long and deep into the earth and reflecting into the stars above the ground. Feel the depth of the nourishing soil, while you rise whole and rich, sourced in a life-supporting cradle of growth.
    Curl your hands and fingers, move your shoulders up and around as the green shoots which unfold into the freedom of sky.
    Choose your leaf patterns. Elect thorns or smooth. Determine vibrancy.
    But you cannot deny the sun, the rising in your veins, arms branching to the heavens in arcs of grace and strength.
    Bridge the worlds of solid and air.
    Choose a color.
    Blaze.

The Sound of Honey

Stepping into the shining of the early morning glow, I taste the fresh color of brightness on the side of my tongue. The blossoming hedges beside the front porch do not feel right until I hear the milling of the bees around me as the day arrives.

With warming sounds increasing in tenor, I begin to sense lemon and rose and honeysuckle; their vibrations soon surround me allowing me to identify location. Clearly able to move along paths once hidden from sight, my senses revel at the depth of the prevalent movement in the air.

The sounds of sweet blossoms stream around me, forcing me to focus and keep my direction lest I be drawn off-course by tempting alien melodies. Like sine waves floating through varying dimensions, I watch bees take off in groups, pairs or single formations, anticipating their turns as they hunt along the singing pollen paths.

I busy with other tasks until the early sun moves to rest upon a drying branch and the weight of the vision above the bushes is suspended for a moment. I blink into new pathways of rising light. As day wings by, I notice the cresting of the light above earth and remain active until the golden globe slips beyond the farthest ridges, eclipsing the sky lanes into twilight.

Settling into silence, I see the stars. Their clarity is keen.

Day's ribboning light fades to silver. The bees fall silent at the approach of night. The moon's shadow brings their flight to a halt; yet in her cool light, I sense the vibration of a low hum far into this reflected darkness.

Finishing a flight of sweetness with you in my dreams, I remain aware of the flare of the brightness within.

It is in these moments of reflection that my stillness comes, as it is in stillness that I find my own reflection.

From a Nest Below the Glacier

White-tufted grebes walk the waters
of a South American lake
until a break allows them to dive,
crack into the lake for a simple supper,
while yet more twangs ring
and air escapes as plates of ice
scrape into each other.

Thawing ice snaps like taut metal wires
popping, clacking on the waves,
and transformed in the heat of the sun,
breaking waters fill the blue lagoons
where we stood this morning
in a landscape laughing
with the bursts of wings,
feathers flapping on ice.

Bubbles leak, and I hear the waters breathe.

Morning moves and the lake
creaks open without its hinges oiled.

Deep toned notes from a wooden flute
roll down the ridges of the moraine
where last night's avalanche fell into stillness.

Today, my sun-crisped skin cries for moisture,
as do my lungs, yet the hidden stars
shooting across the sky
still spell my name
and every muscle
tells me my lessons are over.
Now is the time to fly.

Imagine

Step outside to a place of quiet.

Sit on the ground over there if you'd like. I have an open space beside me, too.

Watch the colors shift across the sky. Are there stars? Is the sunlight unfolding into dawn?

Be aware of clouds, if there are any. What shapes are they in? Can you alter them, asking permission to speak them into different forms?

Observe the land around you. Acknowledge the presence of the hidden folk, even in the city. Talk to them. Express gratitude for their ineffable care of this good earth.

Allow the expansion of thought and the extravagance of creativity to settle within you as you relax into a place of timelessness.

Release concentration without foregoing awareness. Exercise your senses as your mind quiets.

Imagine yourself inside the center of the moon.

You are not there alone. There are many beings, yet taller than all of them is the Grandmother Moon.

As you move toward her, her arms sweep wide with welcome.

She has a place for you.

Listen to her words. Respond with your heart.

Share in the task she gives you and relish the gift of discerning insight.

When you are complete, share your gratitude.

Acknowledge the time to return is now.

Imagine yourself back in your body.

Intensify the feeling of thanks as you amplify the grace of this embodiment with the inhale and exhale of your next breath.

Be mindful of your journey and the intimate lessons you learned. Do something with the message from your experience.

Unwrap the gift of alertness you engaged and with new perception, embrace the world.

Intuit this time.

Be what comes.

17 Inside the Moon

I ride the back of Spirit Hawk, lifting to a distant surface after receiving an open invitation from Grandmother Moon to visit.

The rock throne under the cratered shell is empty. Uncertain how to find her, I kneel and place each hand, fingers widespread, on the surface skin of this celestial body. As soon as I make contact, disturbed moon dust rises up my arms, coating my entire body in a spherical embrace. A tunnel opens before me to the center of the moon. I step forward not knowing what is inside the deepest cavern within the Earth's satellite.

Weightless, I float down a burrowed passage. On one side, I touch a smooth wall of luminescent pearl tones hushed with strokes of pastels. The other side curves in a blue iridescent darkness to meet the paler luster, taking me into a channel where I stop on a ledge overlooking a large interior cavern.

I descend to the bottom of the cave where there are many beings from many different worlds.

The one I know as Grandmother Moon is there, an organizing influence over the activity around her. She welcomes me with smiles and an enveloping embrace, as I express surprise at how many others there are inside the moon.

Grandmother says, "Everyone is here to learn. I have something for you to do if you want to participate."

I join in the activities, even though I wonder what I can do or whether I need special training.

I ask, "Will it involve writing?"

"Do you enjoy writing?," she questions as her eyebrows arch above the violet in her eyes.

I answer, "I love writing–on Earth. Shouldn't I stretch in new ways with so many different things there are to do here?"

Grandmother gazes into my eyes. When she turns to walk away, I move beside her without hesitation.

We lift above the floor and settle in a section of the cavern where I notice open rows in the ground.

She turns to me saying, "Let's find a word that holds great significance for you. Ah, here it is: *peace*."

Grandmother hands me a scrap of a paper-like substance and directs me to write the word peace.

"Isn't that one of your favorite words?"

Nodding, I write with my fingertip, handing the bit of parchment back to her.

I watch as the Grandmother folds the thin slip until it becomes as small as a seed.

Bending over with her, I see her place this tiny object in the closest row of dust, covering it gently as if the word is alive.

As we watch, this planting begins to grow before us, sprouting into a gorgeous, extravagant, strapping, fully-topped shade tree with thick silver leaves, fully formed. I am hooked!

"How much should I write?," I whisper, awed and excited at the same time.

At her gentle look, I discover a group of ten words is adequate for now.

I wait for a moment, sifting through thoughts as Grandmother moves away, and then I write my next word.

Penning the word *love*, I fold this slip of unknown substance into the tiniest seed. While bent to the floor of the cavern, I tuck *love* into the loose regolith around me. I watch this planting grow and notice the dark green lustrous leaves spreading around the cavern like a five-fingered English ivy, covering everything with gentle filaments both tough and smooth to the touch.

I write *melody* on a slip, fold it to seed-size, and plant it farther along the row of moon dust. I smile as this plant grows upward with multiple leaves like staves of music, a different colored stripe to each leaf. Round white blossoms adorn the apex. The simplicity of this bush captivates my heart with blossoming fullness. I set the next seed *harmony* into the ground close to its complement *melody*.

As *harmony* grows, it leans into *melody*, supporting the first plant. Layering leaves under loose clefts and wrapping tendrils of corresponding colors, *harmony* produces a loose mantle around blooms of the single-stemmed *melody* bush. When a whisper of wind blows, these plants sing. As they grow a synergistic companionship, these word plants provide magnificent color dressed with sound.

I write *support* and plant this new word-seed, wondering what it will look like. I marvel as this seed unfolds as a solid mound of purple-tinged maiden grass as tall as my shoulders, full, with strong stems along the entire base of the arching foliage.

Joy is a short penning and another tiny seed, but it sprouts immediately with sunrise blossoms rising like hands, cupping golden liquid light.

When I plant *beauty*, it blossoms under the surface of the moon, spreading out like a light growing just below the top layer of the graying dust. The seeds of *light*, *happy*, and *calm* each grow in their individual plantings, exuding unique qualities of color, sound, and scent as they lift from the ground and climb into the weightless air of the cavern.

When I finish and express my gratitude to the seed words for their wondrous growth, other beings gather to remove the plantings to transplant to their worlds. Each growing seedling goes out with the greatest care, protected with the loving breath of Grandmother Moon.

I thank Grandmother for this experience and am thrilled when she invites me back. Humbled by the work in which I participate, I beam my acceptance of another invitation to learn more of Grandmother's work.

Returning to the surface, ready to fly to Earth, I imagine more words to turn into seeds.

I am ready for more planting.

Looking for Starlight

I kiss a mountain
and where our lips curve
against each other
there opens a crevice
into a cavern of dreams.

Moving into this darkness,
colors fade while senses shift.
I no longer hear the fall of my steps
nor see the separation of my breath.
I no longer smell anything
distinguishing me from the land
cradling my body with benevolent gentleness.

Walking into this passionate Earth,
I discover in our embrace
the origins of my future
in the depths of these ranges,
as I find the seeds of my becoming
mingled among the roots.

Perhaps the buds grow even now.
Maybe they flower on a hillside
yet unexplored, or germinate freely
floating like stars in a river
running under this land,
wet with liquid light
and still, bright promise.

Aligned

Turning, I sit up straight to watch the browned leaves above me toss in the light from the fire. I cannot wait for morning.

I bend my head once more to the flames and to Earth, before lifting my face to the stars. My eyes follow the river of lights in the sky. The horizon is hard to see until I imagine a filter over my eyes which gives me the vision of a nocturnal cat, allowing me to move in the deepest shadows.

I run because I can.

I race straight to the river with three convergent banks and arrive just as you do, just as the sun does, no coincidence. When light crowns the first of the distant mountains, they hum sounding deep under my bare soles. The growing light glows up our already translucent skins. I reach my left hand to connect with your right, and we close our embrace with the rays of the sun.

Bodies connect in a singularly finite and infinite expression. Unexpected. Exhilarating.

The singularity consumes us. In a subtle shift, the extreme brightness we shine breathes with the clarity of ice. Female and male indistinguishable, we merge into one being, lift into air, wrap, bind, loose, caress, release, pulse, and hold.

The pattern repeats with a sense of infinite awareness with lives once lived, relationships remembered and forgotten, reignited and accepted, with accelerating growth. Shaped with a knowledge of returning to wholeness, sufficient to support life in times apart, the breath of our crossing exudes passion sufficient to carry us as we grow.

Together again, our awareness of being alive is elemental.

We feel life in the scent of the dirt, smell the assurance in the bite of the sea, hold the raw burn furrowed into thoughts from hot tears, and see the music of the lightning while hearing the surprise of imagination.

We taste on each other's tongue the nectar of creation.

Ignited energy emanates from everything.

On another level of experience, we lift higher.

I close my eyes to blink, and you are gone.

This time, I recognize your footprints. Without hesitation, I plant my feet next to those indentations beside Tree, raise my hands to the unseen hands that await me, and lift myself into another lifetime where we walk together again.

18 Leaning

This full moon is a good night for leaning.
Stand here beside me, with the light bathing our skin.
Close your eyes. Feel the earth exhale below your feet as you sink into her soil. Expand into the mountain you choose to name.
Feel deep into that mysterious ground of creation.
Allow the breath rising from those darkest caverns to weave through your being, synchronizing your beat with the very heart of the Mother.
Open your eyes to the dancing of ghost lights on tree leaves. Watch as the shimmer rises from the display upon branches, their softened palm leaves, veiled with veins, open to give glow back to the same sky which first coaxed them into the vulnerable skins they wear.
Lift your arms as I lift mine, as we release what we sense in our hands, one palm open to give away and one palm open to receive, balancing the Light within us and the Light without. Hold this position until there is no more thought of otherness; we are simply one conduit for the gift of flow.
Then lean into that space we share where we remember without thought, where we are without being, when separation no longer exists.
We are.
Remember the weaving of this lifetime into memory, past times of forgetfulness and the reawakening of the present.
Recall the joy of original joining.
Lean into me as I lean into you, and relish the gift of awareness.

Dancing in Starlight

Sit here on the porch with me
as we dip our toes
into the star-studded stillness
of rain-damped grass.

Listen to the wind chimes
in the still humid evening
and remember they move
even as we do not.

Let's wade in the vapors
of the Pool of Creation and swim into the swirling
until called by the signature of a star
whose light reverberates against our shining.

We may discover that unbounded awareness—
the essence of star, of light, of being,
greeted and expressing gratitude
for all things.

Notice how it sends us forth,
again, and again, and how our feet
remember to dance among the stars.

Epilogue

Finished with my telling, I step away from the podium.

As I turn to leave the platform, a vibrant figure with amethyst eyes hands me what appears to be a clod of gray dirt. She disappears into the movement around us as easily as she appeared, before I ask any questions.

The color of the soil in my hands reminds me of shades shifting upon a dry, gray planet.

As I look closer at the clump in my hand, it bursts, breaking into the dust from which it was formed. Allowing fine dirt to sift through my fingers, I hold a small piece of folded paper in my palm, remaining from the interior of the clod.

Intrigued, I open the slip, and there appears in my hand a piece of fine luminous fiber on which is written a single word.

With a feeling of wonder, I wrap the parchment into a compact seed.

I look up at the council of Gods stretching across the Known as they share the word pictures of Gaia, content to hear she lives.

Turning away, I face the breath of a breeze pulling my attention away from the present, aware another journey awaits.

Shifting willingly with this familiar spirit, I am ready to be lifted by the Wind after one more task.

Bending over, I scratch a small hole in the ground.

I stay long enough to reach into the indentation below my feet, express simple words of gratitude, and rise after planting the seed *success*.

Stories

This book is not the last of the stories of the descendants of the Chaskakuna and the creation of this world. It may not even be the first.

These tales are their legends, but certainly they are ours as well, for we know them, remember them, and want to belong to them.

Listen to your own stories now.

Awaken.

Recall the space, place and times of beginning.

Tell your narratives out loud. Share their vibrancy.

The stones tell the rest of the story of the wholeness of creation. Pick up a pebble. Hold a precious gem. Tilt your ear to hear its tales.

Taste the comments of life.

Be present with your attention.

Listen to the humming of the mountains. Learn a song of Earth.

We are the descendants of those who came. We never left.

Our roots are with the Beings who traveled here from the stars of that creative void to unite and experience the fullness of our embodied expression.

We begin to remember we are not the caretakers of the garden.

We are the Garden itself.

Chapter Notes

Chapter 2   **Sometimes the Mind Is a Deep Seasonal Storm***   7

*A Response Poem to Jane Hirschfield's
"Sometimes The Heart is a Shallow Autumn River"

Chapter 12   **Unraveling**   58

Reprinted from *Finding Direction*
2013 Finishing Line Press

Acknowledgments

I am grateful to my parents for planting in me a great love of reading and for my deep sense of appreciation for the words we use to create the world around us.

A special word of thanks to my sister, Jan Ronan, whose expertise in editing helped me write in the powerful present. Jan has given countless hours of love in her commitment to the expression of the written word and continues to teach me in ways that both encourage and challenge me to improve my craft.

I am grateful for supportive comments from Dr. Alberto Villoldo, Jose Luis Herrera, Christine Irving, and Dr. Don Vann as well as the time they each spent reading this manuscript. Weekly meetings with poets J. Paul Holcomb, Christine Irving, and Robert Schinzel, whose critiques of my poetry always serve to make me a better poet, continue to improve my writing today. Thank you for sharing your words.

For the shamans with whom I study and continue to improve my perceptions of self and this world, I am deeply grateful.

This book is dedicated especially to my family. Thank you for putting up with my absences as I traveled on inner journeys and on outer explorations in Peru; for reading revisions of poetry and prose; and for your straightforward comments on everything from titles to fonts to early *processes*. Thank you to my children, Stephanie and Kelson, for your understanding as I disappeared into the solo world of writing, and to my husband Randy, for encouraging me with certain confidence that this book would be complete, in order that the next one may be birthed as well.

Glossary

advaita   / ahd•vahē´•tuh /   noun
the teaching of oneness or nonduality
origin: Sanskrit

ayni   / ī´nē /   noun
reciprocity, balance, living in right relationship
origin: Quechua

chaska   / chas´kah /   noun
star
origin: Quechua

Chaskakuna   / chas´kah•koo´nah /   noun
People of the Stars
origin: Quechua

Gaia   / guy´•uh /   noun
in Greek mythology, the earth as a goddess, the daughter of Chaos; a name for Mother Earth
origin: Greek

grebe   / grēb /   noun
a freshwater diving bird
origin: French

k'intu   / kin′too /   noun
three leaves, coca leaves in the Andes, representing the three
worlds—lower, middle and upper - infused with prayers
origin: Quechua

-kuna   / koo′nah /   suffix
makes a singular noun plural
origin: Quechua

paqo   / pa′kō /   noun
a healer or shaman in the Andean tradition
origin: Quechua

prana   / prah′ nah /   noun
the life force or energy permeating the body
origin: Sanskrit

Q'ero   / keh′rō /   noun
Ethnic community of Earthkeepers and healers from the
mountains of Peru
origin: Quechua

regolith   / reg′•o•lith /   noun
layer of loose material (sand, rock, soil, ash, etc.) on the
earth, moon or planet covering the bedrock
origin: Greek and English

Ruh   / rooh /   noun
soul; spirit
origin: Arabic

For Reflections and Insights

Note From the Author

I invite you to contact me with thoughts and reflections after you experience some of the processes written here. Send an email to Beth@TheCalmingCenter.com. I welcome your stories and look forward to learning about the ways you take and make some of these processes uniquely your own.

Please visit me at www.TheCalmingCenter.com and read additional blogs, or contact me for my current schedule of presentations, readings, cleansings, healing ceremonies, and shamanic trainings. I believe we are here to discover our personal fulfillment, and if you are searching for assistance in clearing out what appears to be in the way, please contact me so we can work together to make a difference in your life and that way, in the world.

www.ingramcontent.com/pod-product-compliance
Lightning Source LLC
Chambersburg PA
CBHW032006080426
42735CB00007B/526